From Pain into Purpose

The Memoir Of Prophetess Shavon Foster

Shavon Foster

From Pain to Purpose

John 7:38
He who believes in me, as the scripture has said,
Out of his heart will flow rivers of living water.

Dedication

Thank you all for reading the first of many books to come. I would like to give thanks to my Abba, who is my Father, for gracing me with the wisdom, understanding, and knowledge to complete this segment of my assignment. My Lord and Savior, Jesus Christ, for giving His life for me - that I may live to tell my story (and all that I have encountered) and share my life with the world.

To my mother, Donna Renee Campbell, thank you for pushing me out and pushing me through. She is still pushing even through her death. I am forever loved by you as well as love you.

Also, to my dad, thank you for being who you are and the role you played in this. Because of that, I became a better person.

To all my leaders, I truly thank you for the encounters of life through Christ Jesus with you. To New Life Global Ministry, my Pastor Elder Rodney Richardson, and my lovely First Lady, Gloria Richardson, I love you guys to pieces.

To my siblings, thank you guys for believing in me and loving me for real.

To Author Barbra Owens, thank you for inspiring me to go ahead and write my book. Through your book, I learned I was still hurting and that I needed to uncover some things to recover some things. Thank you so much.

Last but not certainly least, my son - I love you Poopie, my Snookle poodles, for always loving me no matter what and never looking down on me. You're the greatest son any mother could ask for. Thank you for not 'taking me through' or being rebellious. Thank you for being the epitome of a generational curse breaker. I love you, son.

I also want to thank all who played a role and supported me through this walk.

Thank you so much!

Table of Contents

Dedication 3

Chapter One

The Beginning 7

Chapter Two

The Missing Dime 13

Chapter Three

Face to Face with the Devil 17

Chapter Four

The Sickness 23

Chapter Five

The Rebellion Child 35

Chapter Six

He (God) Was Still Working on Me 43

Chapter Seven

The Life of Ecstasy 53

Chapter Eight

Pimps and Strip Clubs.. 57

Chapter One

The Beginning

I have always known that I have a special gift and a special connection to God. As a child, I found myself doing and seeing things that were a bit unusual, although I never understood why. In some odd way, I knew it was a journey, and God was the captain.

My mother shared with me that the enemy was out to kill me from the time I was conceived. The first thing he tried to do was rob me of my identity.

My dad knew that when he and my mother got together, she was a virgin and that she was faithful to him. There was not a problem when my eldest sister was born, their life was peachy, and the union was strong. My sister was well taken care of and loved very deeply by both parents. However, when I was conceived, my dad began to deny me, saying to my mom that he did not want me and that I was not his.

Eventually, my parents split, and as time went on my mother gave birth to me.

Shortly after my birth (about a month or so later), I went into convulsions and died. One of my uncles revived me, saving my life.

The devil was out to kill me, and he never let up.

> The adversary was out to destroy me
> from birth, but God said no!

My mom then shared with me how in the middle of the Chicago winter, she was put out of the house she shared with my grandmother.

The streets were freezing cold. All my mom had was a blanket for me. In an attempt to keep me warm and from freezing to death, she wrapped me in her coat - leaving herself exposed.

She explained to me that by the time she made it to her aunt and uncle's place, she had been frostbitten from the unforgiving Chicago air. Mom told me they had to pry her hands apart to retrieve me!

I cannot say that I remember this family well, but I can say I thank God for His faithful spirit that pressed their hearts to help my mother.

As I grew older, I developed a skin disease called "psoriasis." The disease was so bad that it would cause me to have giant blisters and leave my skin cracked and bleeding from being so dry.

I hated wearing clothes that exposed my skin because people were so unkind. They would mistreat me, talk negatively about me, and point and laugh at me.

The enemy was attacking my self-esteem using the students in my school. It was so bad that I would run home after school and hide in my closet for hours.

*Because others couldn't see my
value, I became an enemy to myself
and developed self-hatred*

In my prayers, I'd ask, "God, why am I here? Why did You allow me to come to this evil place? I did not ask to be here."

I became an enemy to myself and developed self-hatred. I absolutely hated myself – to the point that I could not stand being around myself.

Even though I was having a rough time, I still tried to see the brighter side and believed that eventually people would change to see the good in me.

One day as I was playing outside, a big white bus rode through my Milwaukee, Wisconsin neighborhood asking children if they wanted to go to church.

This was when I started learning a little bit about God. Although I did not fully grasp Him right away, attending services and engaging in the activities for children planted a seed.

God is strategic.

He will use the smallest things, such as arts and crafts, to draw us closer to Him.

This was the first time I had an encounter with God regarding my calling.

Chapter Two

The Missing Dime

One day I was upstairs in my room on the floor playing with a dime, throwing it in the air and catching it before it hit the floor.

I remember that I had done it so much that I had caught a rhythm and didn't have to look up to catch it.

This time, I threw the dime in the air again, but it didn't fall into my hands like it normally did. So, I figured that it must've fallen to the floor. I started searching for my missing dime so that I could continue with the little game I was playing.

I searched behind me, in front of me, and on both sides.

Still no dime.

In one last desperate attempt to locate my missing dime, I got down on all fours to search.

Suddenly, I heard a strong, stern voice call out, "Shavon!"

I looked around but saw no one, so I continued searching for my dime.

Again, I heard the voice call my name, "Shavon!"

I stopped and looked around the room, but this time I responded, "Hunh?"

Then I heard my stepdad (*my dad*) call me by my nickname, "Black Greasy!"

At that very moment, the missing dime fell out of nowhere and landed right in front of me.

I thought to myself, *wow!*

I was frightened and amazed at the same time. I told myself that I would never tell this story because no one would ever believe me.

I still hadn't figured out that God was calling me for a greater purpose, to be His mouthpiece.

I began to have dreams and visions, some of past life and those of the future. Some I could make out, and others I couldn't.

I didn't understand any of it.
Even now, I have visions from God nearly every single day.

It was difficult trying to determine what was real and what was fake while dealing with the children at my school who pointed and laughed at me because of my disability (or shall I say, my disadvantage).

My skin disorder didn't limit me, but it did limit others. They could not see past it.

That time was very hard and challenging.

The devil was trying to assassinate my character before I ever got a glimpse or knowledge of *who* I was or *whose* I was.

But God's plans were bigger than his (the devil)!

Chapter Three

Face to Face with the Devil

When I was in the 4th grade, we moved to Missouri, where I had to change schools. The situation at my new school was not much different than in my previous school. Consequently, I was battling depression and had no desire to attend school.

The children said mean and hateful things about me. No one wanted to be my friend or be seen with me. They would play with me behind closed doors, but not in the eyes of our peers.

Even though I knew it wasn't right, I found myself beholding to those friendships because I desperately wanted to be liked and validated.

While I wasn't technically considered to be handicapped, I was different from others which made them treat me as if I did have a disability. God can use anything for His glory. He gave me compassion for so-called misfits because I was a misfit!

There were these two girls who didn't mind hanging with me and saw no flaw in me.

One was named Elizabeth, and the other was Crystal.

Elizabeth was a bit tall, with red hair and freckles all over her face. Crystal was short and stubby with long black curly hair.

I would take turns going to each one of their homes to play. One day I was at Crystal's home. The enemy tried to introduce himself to me personally!

I will never forget this day, simply because this was the day that Lucifer wanted me to know personally. He wanted me to know that he was closer to me than I ever thought he was!

Crystal and I had gotten out of school. We asked our parents if I could go play at her house.
My mom, seeing how innocent Crystal looked, didn't hesitate to agree and allowed me to go.

Skipping happily down the street, I had no idea what I was about to be exposed to ...

We made it to Crystal's house and began playing with her toys, building a castle, playing princess and dragons, and whatever else our imaginations allowed us to dream of.

I noticed that Crystal's house was really out of order - things were everywhere and very filthy.
It didn't matter to me at the time because this was one of my best friends, and I was happy someone

wanted to be my friend who wasn't ashamed of me.

So, I continued to play as if nothing was wrong and that everything was perfectly fine.

Then out of the blue, she said something that completely blew my mind:

"Shavon, my father is Lucifer," she said.

"Your father is who?" I asked in amazement.

She repeated, "My father is Lucifer."

"OK," I said, "but isn't Lucifer the devil?"

"Yes," she simply replied.

I shook my head back and forth in disbelief. "That's impossible."

She reassured me that Lucifer was her father by explaining to me how it happened.

"Sure, it is," she said. "My mother had sex with him, and they made me. That makes him my father."

"My family believes in and loves God," I told her. "We don't worship the devil."

At that moment, her mom appeared from out of nowhere, and Crystal stopped talking about it.

"My mom can read palms," Crystal said to me. And then to her mom, she said, "Read her palms, Mom."

Her mom immediately grabbed my hands and started telling me about things to come and what would take place in my life.

But she never once mentioned that I had a call of a prophet on my life.

She never mentioned how God would use me to bring His word before people.

She never exposed that God would be great in my life and that one day I would help a generation of people give their lives back to Christ.

However, she did leave a spirit with me that tried to dwell within my body. That was the first encounter with Lucifer, but somehow, I knew it wasn't the last.

Chapter Four

The Sickness

About a week after my encounter with Lucifer trying to introduce himself into my life, I had an illness occur out of the blue.

My stomach was stomach hurting so bad that I couldn't even sit up at my desk.

"I don't feel well," I told my teacher. "I think we should call my mom."

"You're not warm or hot," she said, feeling my forehead.

She refused to call my mom and basically implied that since I wasn't feverish that I didn't have a stomachache.

I ended up regurgitating everywhere.

My mom came and got me from school and took me home. I immediately went to my room and lay in bed, hoping to find some type of relief for the pain I was feeling.

I finally fell asleep.

After sleeping for a few hours, I felt this heavy weight leap on me and woke me instantly.

I remember seeing this female-like figure on top of me, holding my hands and pinning me to the bed. It was so strong that I couldn't move.

I was crying and trying to scream for my mother. My mouth was moving, but no words were coming out.

As I cried, I stared this entity in the face whilst in total fear, not knowing what it was, what it wanted, or why it was even there.

Then heard a voice say, "Pump it, and it will release you."

Using my body, I pumped as hard as I could, and as promised, this evil spirit released me!

Jumping out of bed, I ran as fast as I could to my mom. I was afraid. My heart was beating fast. My eyes were bucked, and I was screaming.

My mom grabbed me and realized my entire body was hot. I had a very high fever and had to be rushed to the hospital, where I was admitted.

The doctors were performing a multitude of tests trying to figure out what was going on with me and why I was so sick.

We were there for a very long time.

And I was so sick that the people who came to visit me had to wear masks and gloves.

I thought it was to keep me from giving them what I had, but I later learned that it was to protect me from their germs.

The doctor asked a strange question: "Have you been in a filthy house or around anyone who was filthy?"

I immediately thought about Crystal's house.

"Yes," I told him. "My friend."

"OK," he said. "Don't go over to her house anymore because you are allergic to filth."

Now that I'm grown, I realize that the devil wanted to live in me, but my body was rejecting him because of the anointing of the Holy Spirit that resides in me.

The Holy Bible states that God can't dwell in an unclean place, surly the devil can't take living in a clean place.

After that, things started turning for the worst for me.

The children were still picking and pointing, laughing, making jokes, and calling me names.

I was growing tired.

I started lashing out at my mom, blaming her for my very existence. I also blamed her for my father not being in my life.

I blamed my mom for this hideous disease that I had to deal with daily.

It was so bad that I didn't want to live.

Thoughts of suicide were strong.

But, in the midst of me contemplating suicide, my mother would call me to her room, or wherever she was at the moment, to teach me about Jesus.

She would tell me about the different encounters she had with God and how she was a missionary who had a gift for seeing the past, present, and future.

I thought, *she must be a psychic, and surely I am too!*

I had to be.

Because I wasn't in church, I had no idea about missionaries, Prophets, Prophetess, or anything of that nature. All I knew was that I was a psychic!

There were countless days of me hearing voices, whispers, and thousands of people talking, whom I couldn't see.

I think I'm going crazy, I thought.

I never shared this with my mom or anyone else for that matter because I felt no one would ever believe me or even understand.

What do you do when you hear the cries of people you don't know or can't see?

I know you all are thinking ... pray.

You're absolutely correct!

Prayer is the answer.

But what if you don't know how to pray or even what to pray?

I was still an adolescent. I didn't have the first clue about praying for myself or others (intercessory prayer).

So, I was left with no hope – a bad attitude and suicidal thoughts.

I was 12 years old thinking, *my dad doesn't want me. My mom hates me because my dad doesn't want me. The kids at school think I'm an alien. I might as well kill myself.*

I grabbed some of my mom's blood pressure pills and took them.

But God ...

Jesus and the Holy Ghost stepped in and blocked them from harming me.

My life was spared, and now I'm able to tell that the anointing of God is real, and He loved me.

All I did was sleep that day.

"Why am I still here, God?" I asked when I woke up. "God, why do You want me here?"

My mom admitted me to St. Joseph's hospital for troubled kids to get me some help but that only made things worse.

Now I was thinking, *she's trying to throw me away. And I need to defend myself. She doesn't like me and is just trying to get rid of me. I'm going to make it worse for them!*

And I did.

I had no idea that all my mother was trying to do was protect me.

There were some kids who lived down the street from us. Their family was some really *churchy* people-sanctified is what they called themselves. They wore long dresses and went to church for what seemed like every day.

One day, I decided that I would go with them.

And while there, I remember the preacher speaking a strong message.

I sat there attentive, listening to every word that flowed from his mouth. My spirit was in tune, and I started to get this feeling that I had never felt before.

In the middle of his preaching, he said, "There is a little girl here who wants to know Jesus. She wants God in her life." He said some other stuff and then continued with, "God is going to use her in a mighty way. And she will be a great woman of God."

As the words flowed from him, I knew he was talking about me. I was afraid and excited at the same time. My palms were sweaty, my hands were shaking, and I wanted to leap.

This was the first time that I experienced the Holy Spirit.

Chapter Five

The Rebellion Child

Back to me wanting to commit suicide and being placed in Saint Joseph Hospital ...

After getting out of the hospital, I had already made up my mind that I was going to make things worse for my mother for trying to get rid of me.

When I got out of the hospital, my mom had moved to Arkansas, where I met this girl who was affiliated with a gang called *Up-Gangster Disciples/Growth development.*

I decided that I would join this gang so that I could have people behind me, a place where I belonged. Be mindful of the fact that I am living

35

in a home where my siblings have alienated me. I felt like I didn't belong there, and so I was looking for love - just any kind of love.

I just needed to be loved. I longed to be loved.

Consequently, I was looking for love in any place and at any expense - it didn't matter. I just needed to feel something because I had been numb for so long.

Any type of feeling was plenty for me.

The gain was offering me what I thought I wanted from them – love and acceptance. So, I joined the gang.

My superior taught me how to be part of this family. I was taught the things I needed to do and the procedures I needed to follow to become part of their so-called *family*.

This is where things were getting bad and going downward.

I became promiscuous - sleeping with different men to get attention from them just to feel a feeling.

This led me to my son's father, a man who would teach me what it was like to be abused and beaten by love (or so I thought). He would be just the first of many encounters with abusive relationships.

There were times when I would be lying in bed, and as soon as I woke up, he would hit me for no reason!

Or I would be in the store, walking around looking for items, and as soon as I returned home from the store, he would beat me.

Sometimes, it felt like he beat me just because it was Tuesday or the day seemed like a great day to beat me. There was no reasoning.

At this point, I thought that this was love.

It had to be because I could feel it (love) even though it hurt. This *had to* be what it meant to be loved.

If he hit me, that meant he loved me.

I thought it was normal behavior, and soon if I wasn't being beaten, I didn't feel like I was being loved.

In my mind, pain was an indicator of love - not that something was wrong.

I had no clue what *real* love felt like, so any type of feeling to me was love

Because I was so numb and I wanted to be loved so badly, I was willing to endure any type of behavior that even *remotely* resembled someone caring for me.

Men beating me was such normal behavior.

It was so bad that I would purposely anger them so they would beat me and I would then feel loved!

I had no idea that I had a problem. In my heart, I believed this was normal.

I saw my mom being abused by my dad.

Surely, since my dad loved my mom, and if he beat her, then the man that I got with must beat me too if he loved me.

Sadly, this was the only way I knew that love was expressed.

But the devil is a liar.

I had some growing up to do and some soul-searching too.

Trying to find myself, I moved to Tennessee, where I learned that I was pregnant with my son.

Again, I have to go through being laughed at (the hurt place) because I am now a pregnant teen.

The parents of my schoolmates didn't want me at the school because I was too young to be pregnant. I was a bad influence.

And again, I am cast away from society.

I found myself back in the midst of feeling unwanted.
But at the same time, I was thanking God that He had given me what I'd asked Him for – someone who would love me no matter what I was, what I

looked like, what type of skin I had, how much money I had, or what kind of car I drove.

None of that would matter.

I knew that this child would love me without a shadow of a doubt. I was so happy. I was so excited to be having a baby.

I had to pretend as if I wasn't excited and that I was ashamed in front of my mom because I didn't want to disappoint my mom.

But in the same breath, I wanted to be pregnant because it meant that I would have something I could call my own and someone who would love me for real.

God gave that to me. He gave me my son.

I still hadn't learned about God and what He'd done for me back on Calvary's Cross.

Therefore, the saga continued. It was nowhere near over. There were more things to be faced and more pain I needed to go through to reach my purpose.

Chapter Six

He (God) Was Still Working on Me

Everything seemed to be going OK.

It was May. My son was getting older; he would turn one soon. His father and I were together, and everything appeared to be going good.

Then suddenly, I began to get sick again. This time I was so sick that I started losing weight really fast.

I remember going to the doctor or hospital every week or every other week.

I was sick all the time.

The doctors were trying to determine what was wrong with me.

They thought I had Hepatitis and some other type of sickness. So, they ran all these different tests on me, and I found out that my bowels were moving in the wrong direction.

They were going upwards instead of downwards!

I had to have emergency surgery to remove the bow from my system.

Later, we learned that my son's father had given me chlamydia. I hadn't had any symptoms and didn't realize I had the disease. All I knew was that I was quickly fading away.

My doctor confirmed that I was losing weight rapidly and close to death!

While I was fighting for my life, my mom was admitted to the hospital for a heart attack.

She called my auntie and asked her how I was doing.

"She isn't doing too well," My aunt said. "It doesn't look good."

My mom had a vision, or maybe God spoke to her.

"Tell her the Lord said if she doesn't get up out of that hospital bed, she will be dead by the next morning." She told my aunt. "And I'll be burying my daughter."

Sick herself, my mom got up from her bed, snatched the cords that had her attached to the machines, and rushed home from Memphis.

She took me to the hospital.

After two days of being in the hospital, I had a visit from the devil.

He spoke to me these very words:

"I got you," he said. "I finally got you."

I remember screaming:

"You don't have me. You don't have me."

I pressed the button for the nurse to come in.

Then I took the Gideon Bible out of the drawer next to the bed. I turn the T.V. to TBN (Turner Broadcast Network). There were two people talking about God and his goodness.

Those two people were Andre and Jan Crouch.

The nurse came in.

I was shouting, "Can you see him?" I asked, shaking now too. "Can you see him? He is sitting right there! He said he finally got me. I told him he doesn't have me. Tell him he doesn't have me," I pleaded. "Tell him!"

The nurse looked where I was pointing.

"There is no one there," she said, rubbing my hand. "It's just the meds. They have you hallucinating."

But she was looking right at him!

The nurse's name was Lisa. I will never forget her. She was an older Caucasian woman with hair so gray that it looked snow white. She was average size and height.

As she continued to rub my hand, this sense of calm fell over my body.

"He doesn't exist," she kept repeating.

And when I looked back over towards him, he had disappeared.

I told my mom about it.

"I saw him," she said. "It was the spirit realm and prayer fighting against him."

I was so amazed and relieved! I thought that I was tripping and that *maybe* I *was* crazy.

But this was another failed attempt by the devil to kill me.

Later, when another nurse came to check my vitals, I asked about Nurse Lisa.

"There was no nurse here by that name last night."

And I knew right then that this was an Angel.

Not too long after the last incident, I got into a little trouble with the police, where there was this big altercation that landed me with a 2nd-degree felony charge - an assault against a police officer.

In 1999, I took a plea bargain for fighting the cops, which landed me a 2nd-degree battery charge for assault against a police officer.

As I revisit this horrific time in my life, I think about how God shielded and protected me.

That officer could have shot me dead!

Instead, God gave me another chance to get it right.

Thank you, Jesus!

However, getting it right was still very far from where I was standing then.

I had gotten permission from the state of Arkansas to move to Minneapolis, Minnesota, to start my new life - which was another way of escaping who I once was.

I Thought for sure I was going to head in the right direction for betterment, but the enemy wasn't playing and definitely was not letting up.

Things were going OK in the beginning.

I started Summit Academy in hopes of obtaining a Microsoft Word, Excel, and PowerPoint certification.

I just knew I would finish this course, but that didn't happen.

By the time I turned 22, I had decided that I pursue becoming a rapper.

I did that for a little while, dragging my son with me, up all night in the studio trying to make music and become the next female hip hop artist.

But God had other plans for me.

The Bible declares, *my thoughts are not your thoughts, nor my ways are your ways.*

Jer. 29:11 states *For I know the plans that I think towards you that are good and not of evil to bring you to an expected end.*

I'm still reaching for that expected end.

Chapter Seven

The Life of Ecstasy

I spent countless nights in the studio.

Minutes became hours. Hours became days.

I was living a life of liquor, drugs, and sex.

So much so until my body had become immune, and I needed more to get me higher.

That is when I was introduced to ecstasy.

This drug could be an upper or a downer - depending upon what you were doing. Whatever you are feeling at the time you take the drug, you feel it ten times more after taking it.

So, if you were up and hyper, you became ten times more hyper. If you were down and depressed, that is what you'd feel for the rest of the night.

In other words, you had to be mindful of your feelings before taking ecstasy.

Ecstasy is also called 'the truth drug' rumored to be used by the U.S. Army on their enemies to make them tell all.

And yes, you will tell all.

I would take this drug and be up for days at a time, thinking, *I'm going to be the next Brat, Eve, Queen Latifiah or Gansta Boo.*

Little did I know, I was in for a rude awakening.

Things got so bad; that I wouldn't know where my next meal was coming from.

But can I tell you that God still provided for me during my mess and rebellious lifestyle?

I remember walking down the north side street of Minneapolis with my son, hungry and thinking, *God, I need you to make a way.*

And I look up and see a twenty-dollar bill lying on the ground in a fenced-in yard.

Or another time, two women from a ministry of some sort came up to me and asked if I would like to sign up for something that had to do with their ministry.

I did what they asked and was given a gift of coupons for free food from McDonald's.

I remember being so grateful for the blessings but still hadn't yet truly recognized the Blesser.

A thought entered my mind, *this rapping isn't paying me right now, and I need some money.*

I go on to be introduced to something that could only be described as the thing that can bring you straight to the fiery gates of hell!

Chapter Eight

Pimps and Strip Clubs

I needed money.

I had no real work experience and needed a way to make some money - quick.

A friend of mine had told me about some things that I never knew about or ever thought that I would ever do.

She explained to me she knew how to make some money. She had run an ad in the newspaper about being a massage therapist or a masseuse

"All you have to do, "she explained, "is run the ad, and that's how you get customers or clients."

I later learned I also had to provide a 'happy ending.'

Men would come to get a massage, and I'd be expected to *do a little something* that would make them *happy* in the end.

No harm, no foul, I thought.

But later, I go on to meet some pimps, and this is where it goes from bad to worse. Before I know it, I'm taking trips to Chicago, Atlantic City, New Jersey, Atlanta, and Las Vegas.

So much happens in these cities that blew my mind. Now that I look back on it, I should have been afraid.

But at the time, I was just trying to survive.

You'll have to read my next book to find out what happened. Stay tuned.

Learn to write down
what you see and hear
as a prophet

THIS
Prophetic Journal
BELONGS TO:

_____

_____

_____

Delight yourself in the Lord,
and he will give you the
desires of your heart.

Psalm 37:4

Date:

_____

Daily Scripture or Inspiration

Prayers

_____
_____
_____
_____
_____
_____
_____
_____

Prophetic Visions

My Thoughts

_____
_____
_____
_____

Date:

_____

Daily Scripture or Inspiration

Prayers

_____
_____
_____
_____
_____
_____
_____
_____

Prophetic Visions

My Thoughts

_____
_____
_____
_____

Date:
_____

Daily Scripture or Inspiration

Prayers

_____
_____
_____
_____
_____
_____
_____

Prophetic Visions

My Thoughts

_____
_____
_____
_____

Date:
_____

Daily Scripture or Inspiration

Prayers

_____
_____
_____
_____
_____
_____
_____
_____
_____

Prophetic Visions

My Thoughts

_____
_____
_____
_____

Date:
_____

Daily Scripture or Inspiration

Prayers

_____
_____
_____
_____
_____
_____
_____
_____
_____

Prophetic Visions

My Thoughts

_____
_____
_____
_____

Date:

_____

Daily Scripture or Inspiration

Prayers

_____
_____
_____
_____
_____
_____
_____

Prophetic Visions

My Thoughts

_____
_____
_____
_____

Date:

_____

Daily Scripture or Inspiration

Prayers

_____
_____
_____
_____
_____
_____
_____

Prophetic Visions

My Thoughts

_____
_____
_____
_____

Date:
_____

_____ Daily Scripture or Inspiration _____

Prayers

_____
_____
_____
_____
_____
_____
_____
_____

Prophetic Visions

My Thoughts

_____
_____
_____
_____

Date:

_____

Daily Scripture or Inspiration

Prayers

_____
_____
_____
_____
_____
_____
_____
_____

Prophetic Visions

My Thoughts

_____
_____
_____
_____

Date:
_____

Daily Scripture or Inspiration

Prayers

_____
_____
_____
_____
_____
_____
_____
_____

Prophetic Visions

My Thoughts

_____
_____
_____
_____

Date:
_____

Daily Scripture or Inspiration

Prayers

_____
_____
_____
_____
_____
_____
_____
_____

Prophetic Visions

My Thoughts

_____
_____
_____
_____

Date:
_____

Daily Scripture or Inspiration

Prayers

_____
_____
_____
_____
_____
_____
_____
_____

Prophetic Visions

My Thoughts

_____
_____
_____
_____

Date:
_____

Daily Scripture or Inspiration

Prayers

_____
_____
_____
_____
_____
_____
_____
_____

Prophetic Visions

My Thoughts

_____
_____
_____
_____

Date:
_____

Daily Scripture or Inspiration

Prayers

_____
_____
_____
_____
_____
_____
_____
_____
_____

Prophetic Visions

My Thoughts

_____
_____
_____
_____

Date:

Daily Scripture or Inspiration

Prayers

Prophetic Visions

My Thoughts

Date:

_____

Daily Scripture or Inspiration

Prayers

_____
_____
_____
_____
_____
_____
_____
_____

Prophetic Visions

My Thoughts

_____
_____
_____
_____

Date:
_____

Daily Scripture or Inspiration

Prayers

_____
_____
_____
_____
_____
_____
_____
_____
_____

Prophetic Visions

My Thoughts

_____
_____
_____
_____

Date:

Daily Scripture or Inspiration

Prayers

Prophetic Visions

My Thoughts

Date:

_____

_____ Daily Scripture or Inspiration _____

Prayers

_____
_____
_____
_____
_____
_____
_____
_____

Prophetic Visions

My Thoughts

_____
_____
_____
_____

Date:
_____

Prayers

_____
_____
_____
_____
_____
_____
_____
_____

Prophetic Visions

My Thoughts

_____
_____
_____
_____

Date:
_____

Daily Scripture or Inspiration

Prayers

_____
_____
_____
_____
_____
_____
_____
_____

Prophetic Visions

My Thoughts

_____
_____
_____
_____

Date:
_____

Daily Scripture or Inspiration

Prayers

_____
_____
_____
_____
_____
_____
_____
_____

Prophetic Visions

My Thoughts

_____
_____
_____
_____

Date: _____

_____ Daily Scripture or Inspiration _____

Prayers

_____
_____
_____
_____
_____
_____
_____
_____
_____

Prophetic Visions

My Thoughts

_____
_____
_____
_____

Date:

_____

Daily Scripture or Inspiration

Prayers

_____
_____
_____
_____
_____
_____
_____
_____
_____

Prophetic Visions

My Thoughts

_____
_____
_____
_____

Date:
_____

Daily Scripture or Inspiration

Prayers

_____
_____
_____
_____
_____
_____
_____
_____

Prophetic Visions

My Thoughts

_____
_____
_____
_____

Date:

_____

—————— Daily Scripture or Inspiration ——————

Prayers

_____
_____
_____
_____
_____
_____
_____
_____

Prophetic Visions

My Thoughts

_____
_____
_____
_____

Date:
_____

Daily Scripture or Inspiration

Prayers

_____
_____
_____
_____
_____
_____
_____
_____

Prophetic Visions

My Thoughts

_____
_____
_____
_____

Date:

_____

Daily Scripture or Inspiration

Prayers

_____
_____
_____
_____
_____
_____
_____
_____

Prophetic Visions

My Thoughts

_____
_____
_____
_____

Date:
_____

Daily Scripture or Inspiration

Prayers

_____
_____
_____
_____
_____
_____
_____
_____

Prophetic Visions

My Thoughts

_____
_____
_____
_____

Date: _____

Daily Scripture or Inspiration

Prayers

_____
_____
_____
_____
_____
_____
_____
_____

Prophetic Visions

My Thoughts

_____
_____
_____
_____

Date:
_____

Daily Scripture or Inspiration

Prayers

_____
_____
_____
_____
_____
_____
_____
_____

Prophetic Visions

My Thoughts

_____
_____
_____
_____

Date:

_____

Daily Scripture or Inspiration

Prayers

_____
_____
_____
_____
_____
_____
_____
_____

Prophetic Visions

My Thoughts

_____
_____
_____
_____

Date: _____

Daily Scripture or Inspiration

Prayers

_____
_____
_____
_____
_____
_____
_____
_____

Prophetic Visions

My Thoughts

_____
_____
_____
_____

Date:
_____

Daily Scripture or Inspiration

Prayers

_____
_____
_____
_____
_____
_____
_____
_____

Prophetic Visions

My Thoughts

_____
_____
_____
_____

Date:

Daily Scripture or Inspiration

Prayers

Prophetic Visions

My Thoughts

Date:

_____

Daily Scripture or Inspiration

Prayers

_____
_____
_____
_____
_____
_____
_____
_____

Prophetic Visions

My Thoughts

_____
_____
_____
_____

Date: _____

Daily Scripture or Inspiration

Prayers

Prophetic Visions

My Thoughts

Date:
_____

Daily Scripture or Inspiration

Prayers

_____
_____
_____
_____
_____
_____
_____
_____
_____

Prophetic Visions

My Thoughts

_____
_____
_____
_____

Date:
_____

Daily Scripture or Inspiration

Prayers

_____
_____
_____
_____
_____
_____
_____

Prophetic Visions

My Thoughts

_____
_____
_____
_____

Date: _____

Daily Scripture or Inspiration

Prayers

_____
_____
_____
_____
_____
_____
_____
_____

Prophetic Visions

My Thoughts

_____
_____
_____
_____

Date:

_____

Daily Scripture or Inspiration

Prayers

_____
_____
_____
_____
_____
_____
_____
_____

Prophetic Visions

My Thoughts

_____
_____
_____
_____

Date:
_____

Daily Scripture or Inspiration

Prayers

_____
_____
_____
_____
_____
_____
_____
_____

Prophetic Visions

My Thoughts

_____
_____
_____
_____

Date:
_____

Daily Scripture or Inspiration

Prayers

_____
_____
_____
_____
_____
_____
_____
_____
_____

Prophetic Visions

My Thoughts

_____
_____
_____
_____
_____

Notes

Notes

Notes

Notes

Notes

Notes

Notes

Notes

Notes

Notes

Notes

For the Lord is righteous,
he loves justice;
the upright will see his
face.

Psalm 11:7

AUTHOR SHAVON FOSTER

Shavon foster native of Osceola Arkansas. God has given her a great role as a mother in the life of her child. She's a prophetess, life coach, minister and now an author for God. Foster received God in her life and was given the charge to bring forth deliverance by her personal testimony that proceeds from her life lived. The fire of God releases from her womb and breaks forth into the lives of everyone she comes in contact with.

Welcome

My husband Charles and I are the founders of Living Water Books Christian Publishing Company. I always knew from my childhood that I was chosen to record (write) for God. The prophetic gift rested upon my mother. My father told me I had the spiritual gift, but I needed to learn the skill, so he admonished me to pursue a higher education. I began college courses while in high school and three years later I received my B.A. Degree in Mass Communications with a concentration in News Editorial, Broadcasting, and Journalism. I met my husband and a few years later I released my first book, A Heart Unraveled, which I self-published. It became a best-seller allowing us to travel doing conferences, interviews, and book signings.

God established our business on the foundations of (John 7:38), Whoever believes in me, as scripture has said, rivers of living water will flow from within them. Living Water being symbolic for Holy Spirit living within us became the Living Waters within our writings as we prepared resources for our marriage ministry. Holy Spirit splashed through the pages and the testimonies that derived from the resources told us what we needed to do next. We looked at one another and said the name will be, Living Water Books.

Founders of Living Water Books Publishing Company

Visit our website Livingwaterbooks.org

> Living Water Books is God's company. The Living Water of God into books distributed all over the world. God chose us as stewards and we are committed to serving God's Kingdom through God's people.

Living Water Books

Living Water Books
John 7:38

CONTACT US TODAY

THE CHRISTIAN

PUBLISHING COMPANY